W9-CGN-895

large print
SUDOKU

PAPP Puzzles™

Visit our website to find
more quality products:
www.pappintl.com

Copyright © 2018 PAPP International Inc. Printed in China. All rights reserved.
No part of this book may be reproduced or copied in any manner without prior
written permission from the publisher. For more information, contact us at
info@pappintl.com or write to us at:

PAPP International Inc.
177 Merizzi Street, Montreal (Quebec),
CANADA H4T 1Y3

ONE TREE PLANTED

A portion of the proceeds from the sale of this book
goes toward reforestation and the Million Tree Challenge.

www.onetreeplanted.org

HOW TO SOLVE A SUDOKU PUZZLE

Each Sudoku puzzle consists of a 9-by-9 grid of numbers that has been partly filled in. The goal is to fill in all the remaining empty squares so that each row, each column, and each "box" contains all of the numbers from 1 to 9.

4	1	6	9	7	2	8	5	3
3	5	7	1	6	8	2	9	4
9	8	2	5	3	4	1	7	6
7	4	3	2	8	6	5	1	9
5	6	9	3	1	7	4	2	8
8	2	1	4	5	9	3	6	7
2	9	5	6	4	3	7	8	1
6	7	4	8	2	1	9	3	5
1	3	8	7	9	5	6	4	2

ROW

Each row must contain the numbers 1, 2, 3, 4, 5, 6, 7, 8, and 9.

COLUMN

Each column must contain the numbers 1, 2, 3, 4, 5, 6, 7, 8, and 9.

BOX

Each Sudoku consists of 9 "boxes." As with each row and column, each box must contain the numbers 1, 2, 3, 4, 5, 6, 7, 8, and 9.

PUZZLE 1

		6		2				5
			4		1			6
	9				8	4	3	2
9	3				4			
			3	1	5			
			7				4	8
4	5	3	8				2	
2			5		9			
8				3		5		

EASY

PUZZLE 2

2			3		9		6	
	5			8				
	3		2			4		
	8	3		5	6	2	4	
		7	9		2	3		
	4	2	8	3		5	9	
		1		3			2	
				2			5	
	2		6		8			3

EASY

PUZZLE 3

	1			5		3	8	7
			8		4	2		6
							9	
	3	6				7		9
	9			6			3	
7		4				6	5	
	4							
9		2	4		1			
6	8	1		2			4	

EASY

4		3	9				7	5
		5			4			
6	8			7		9		
2			5					
	5		4	9	2		1	
					8			9
		4		5			3	8
			8			2		
8	3				9	7		6

EASY

PUZZLE 5

2	6	1					9	
	4							
	8	5		2	1			
7	2	6	1				5	
5			2		4			9
	1			6	2	3	7	
			4	6		9	2	
							7	
	9				5	4	1	

EASY

PUZZLE 6

	5			9				3
			5				9	6
	9			3		4	5	
3	6	4			7			
2			8		5			4
			3			2	6	7
	1	6		5		3		
9	4				6			
5				8			4	

EASY

PUZZLE 7

	2			5		4		9
			7			2	5	1
	6				2		8	
2				6		5	1	
5								6
	8	6		1				2
	5		4				2	
3	1	7			5			
8		2		3			9	

EASY

PUZZLE 8

					9		3	
	4			1		5		8
		5		2		6		
4	6			9			1	5
1				4				3
5	3			2			7	4
	2		6		4			
6		1		5			4	
	9		2					

EASY

PUZZLE 9

				7		3		
6	4		3					1
8			4					
7		1	8			2		9
	8	2		3		6	7	
9		6			2	8		4
					7			2
2					5		9	3
		8		4				

EASY

PUZZLE 10

	8			4			5	
9			2	7	8		3	
		6				8	4	
		2	7			1		
6				2				3
		3			1	5		
	3	8				4		
	4		5	8	2			6
	6			1			9	

EASY

PUZZLE 11

4	1		5					
9		8		4		7	6	5
3		7						
						5		8
		5	4	6	8	1		
8		1						
						8		6
1	6	4		8		3		7
					1		4	9

EASY

PUZZLE 12

9		1			2		7	3
	3					6	1	5
	9	8	2	1		4		
7				6				1
		6		9	7	5	3	
5	6	3					4	
1	8		5			7		6

EASY

PUZZLE 13

2		5	3					7
4	1			6	7			
			5	2		8		
1		4				3	6	
		6				9		
	5	3				7		1
		2		5	9			
			6	8			5	9
5				3		6		8

EASY

PUZZLE 14

		4				1		
			5		1	2	4	8
2					8			
6					7	3		4
4			6	2	5			7
7		8	1					5
			2					1
1	4	7	8		3			
		9				5		

EASY

PUZZLE 15

		1	2		6		8	
	7						4	3
		5			3	2		
7			6		5	1		
5	1						7	4
		8	4		1			6
		3	9			4		
9	5						6	
	8		1		4	9		

EASY

PUZZLE 16

			8	1		7		
7	4				6	8		
			7	4			2	9
	9	4		6				8
	1						7	
8			3		9	6		
1	6		4	9				
		2	6				1	5
		8		5	7			

EASY

	3		4	2		9		6
4		7	8			1		
	1	9	2			5		8
		2	7		5	4		
6		4			3	7	2	
		6			8	2		7
2		8		7	6		9	

EASY

PUZZLE 18

	7			2		6		
9			7					3
6	8	5	1			2		9
8								
1		4	3	7		6		
						3		
6		2		5	9	7	4	
8					4		2	
	7		8			5		

EASY

PUZZLE 19

				6				
	5					4	6	
2		6			7	3	5	8
	6	5				2		4
	9		4		8		5	1
3			8			7	9	
5	7	3	6			9		2
	8	9					3	
				3				

EASY

PUZZLE 20

	5	1	8	9				
						1	5	
	6		5	1		3	2	
		7		8	9			
	8		5		2			
	7	3		4				
1	4		7	2			3	
8	5							
		8	5		7	1		

EASY

PUZZLE 21

1	7	6		3		2		8
				2	6		7	3
			8					
	1					5		4
		2		6		3		
7		9					1	
					8			
8	6		2	1				
4		1		9		8	3	5

EASY

PUZZLE 22

7				8		2	3	
						9	7	4
	2	4	9		7			
4	9	8						
	3			9			2	
						8	1	9
			1		4	5	8	
2	1	3						
	4	5		3			9	

EASY

PUZZLE 23

		6	2	5		4		
		1			8		2	
4					3	9	5	
					5			
9	3	5		6		8	4	2
			3					
	5	9	1					4
	8		9			5		
		2		8	6	1		

EASY

PUZZLE 24

	8		9		3		7	
5								3
	3	9	7				8	2
						2	5	1
	5		1		9		4	
1	2	8						
3	7				5	9	2	
8								7
	1		2		7		6	

EASY

PUZZLE 25

	1				4			9
	9		3	2				
	8		7	9	1			
				1	6	5		
4	5	9			2		1	3
	7	5	4					
			1	6	5		2	
				3	9		5	
4			2				9	

EASY

PUZZLE 26

		3		2				1
	7					8	2	9
	9		7	1			6	3
		9	6					7
	3						9	
7					2	6		
3	8			4	7		1	
4	6	2					3	
9				3		2		

EASY

PUZZLE 27

						8		
		6	2	4			1	
	2		7					5
2			1		5	4		
		1				2		
		4	8		6			3
1					8		9	
	3			1	7	5		
		7						

MEDIUM

			6					4
				2			8	3
		4			1		6	
		3			2			
6			4		5			2
			7			5		
	7		1			2		
3	6			8				
1				3				

MEDIUM

		1	2	7			9	
4					1	2		8
					3	6		
1				5				
	6		9				4	
			6					9
		2	7					
3		5	8					2
	1			5	2	3		

MEDIUM

PUZZLE 30

6	5					8	7	
					4			
	2	7				4		
2	7		9		1			
	1	4		2	6			
		6		3		2	9	
	3				7	6		
		3						
	6	2					1	4

MEDIUM

PUZZLE 31

	6						3	2
		1	8					
2	4				5	8		
		8	7					
	9	4	2			8	1	7
					9	6		
		2	5				1	4
					7	3		
9	1						5	

MEDIUM

PUZZLE 32

			5	3	4		9	
		5						
3	4			7		2		
	7	6		2				5
5								3
8				5		6	4	
	2			4			6	9
						3		
	6		3	8	1			

MEDIUM

PUZZLE 33

	2	3			7	9	8	
			4			7	5	2
				8				
		8		7				1
1								9
7				4		5		
			5					
8	4	5				6		
	7	6	9			8	4	

MEDIUM

PUZZLE 34

	6					7		5
					3		1	
		7	5		6			9
			2			1		6
			1		7			
3		2			5			
8			6		4	2		
	4		9					
1		6					7	

MEDIUM

	4							2
			8			7		
5		6	7	3			9	
	7		9		4			8
				6				
9			2		7		4	
	9			2	1	6		7
	4			8				
6							8	

MEDIUM

PUZZLE 36

			9					6
	5		3				8	4
1	3		4	6				
	1	6						5
2						9	3	
				5	9		6	7
8	6				2		5	
5					4			

MEDIUM

PUZZLE 37

9				8				
		1	5	6	3	7		
	7							
		6		3		8		1
2								6
7		8		4		5		
							2	
		7	4	2	6	9		
				9				3

MEDIUM

PUZZLE 38

7			3	1				
1	9		4				7	
	4			7	5			
	1	9				7		
5								2
		2				9	1	
			8	5			4	
	3				7		5	1
				2	4			8

MEDIUM

PUZZLE 39

1					9			
8	3		5					1
	7		1	3			8	2
						1	5	4
4	1	9						
5	8			1	3		4	
7					8		1	5
			9					6

MEDIUM

PUZZLE 40

5					6	2		
9					3			
		1			7			
	3				8		5	
1	6						8	2
	5		2				7	
			8			3		
			1					9
		2	3					4

MEDIUM

PUZZLE 41

		6		5		8	
7			8					
		4	6	1		2		
				9				7
3								2
8			3					
		8		7	3	9		
					4			1
	7		2			4		

MEDIUM

PUZZLE 42

	9			6				3
	4				1			
		1	8		4			
7					5			9
		8				2		
9			7					5
			9		2	3		
			3				2	
6				4			9	

MEDIUM

PUZZLE 43

			6		9		2	
4		6				8	1	
	7				5			
	2	3					9	1
			2		3			
9	6					4	3	
			4				8	
	8	4				3		9
	3		9		6			

MEDIUM

PUZZLE 44

	8				3	7		
2			9					
5				1	8	4		
	7					3	8	
	3	9					1	
		2	5	9				3
					4			7
		6	2				5	

MEDIUM

PUZZLE 45

5					1		9	
			9					
	9				5	2	8	6
	7				9	1		4
				2				
6		1	8				7	
7	6	3	5				2	
					6			
	8		3					1

MEDIUM

PUZZLE 46

	2	3		8				
6	5						2	
			9		2			
9					1	4		
3	4						9	6
		5	6					3
			8		4			
	7						5	4
			7			1	6	

MEDIUM

PUZZLE 47

		2				4		
		8		2	9			
5	7			1				8
9	1							6
		4				7		
8							5	1
2				5			8	4
			2	9		5		
		1				6		

MEDIUM

PUZZLE 48

		2	9	8				
			4				5	
				1		6		8
8					5	1	7	
5				4				6
	1	6	8					3
3		5		2				
	7				4			
				5	9	2		

MEDIUM

PUZZLE 49

	3		8				2	9
		2						
			9			5	1	3
		8	5	6				
9			7		4			5
				8	2	7		
3	4	6			7			
						1		
2	1				8		6	

MEDIUM

PUZZLE 50

		4			7		5	
3				8		7		9
		8			2			
		1					4	6
	6	9				5	7	
7	3					9		
			8			1		
9		7		3				5
	4		7			2		

MEDIUM

PUZZLE 51

	7					2		4
2		1		8		3		6
	5	2						
					6			8
	8			2			3	
9			4					
					9	8		
8		3		4		6		7
5		9					4	

MEDIUM

PUZZLE 52

	3							
	7		4	6		9	2	
					2	7	3	
				3				8
		4	7		1	3		
2				8				
	2	7	6					
	6	9		1	7		5	
							4	

MEDIUM

PUZZLE 53

		2	6			7		
						3		1
			9	4	6	5		
9						1		
6			2		5			7
	4							3
	2	5	8	3				
3		7						
		6			7	5		

MEDIUM

PUZZLE 54

7		9			4			
				3			1	
		6		9				7
	7		2			1		
3								2
		1			7		6	
9				5		2		
	8		7					
			6			4		1

EXPERT

PUZZLE 55

			1			7	3	
					3	1		6
				4			2	
9		6	7		8			
3								7
			2		6	9		8
	4			1				
1		9	6					
	6	8			2			

EXPERT

PUZZLE 56

			8			5		
								7
		1		9		2	4	
1			6		4	3		5
		8				4		
6		4	5		9			2
	1	9		4		8		
7								
		2			1			

EXPERT

PUZZLE 57

		7	8			3		
	3		4				8	
				6		9	5	
			9			4		
6				3				8
		5			1			
	5	3		1				
	9				4		1	
		1			2	5		

EXPERT

PUZZLE 58

		9						6
4	5		2	3		9		
					5			7
	4	8		6				
9								5
				5		8	2	
7			3					
		6		2	7		4	8
8						5		

EXPERT

PUZZLE 59

	1	5					7	
		7		5				1
6					3	4		
					7		3	8
	8					9		
4	6		8					
		6	3					9
5				2		3		
	9					5	8	

EXPERT

PUZZLE 60

			9	3	6		
			7		6		2	
9	3		4					
	5					4	1
8								6
3	4				8			
				7			1	5
6		2		5				
	9	3	4				

EXPERT

PUZZLE 61

1	5	6				4		
		8						
7	4				2		1	
		4	6					8
			2		9			
8				1	3			
	7		1				5	9
						6		
		2				1	3	4

EXPERT

PUZZLE 62

	1				2		9	7
							6	
7			5	6		1		
					1			5
8	9						2	4
5			2					
		6		8	9			1
	7							
1	5		6				4	

EXPERT

PUZZLE 63

				7				
		2	1					7
	8		6	3	5		9	
		1						6
	2		8		9		5	
3						8		
	1		4	5	6		3	
2					8	4		
				1				

EXPERT

PUZZLE 64

			9	6	4			
							3	
1					8			6
7		6	2			4		
8		4				2		9
		9			3	7		5
9			4					2
	8							
			5	3	9			

EXPERT

PUZZLE 65

		8					5	
2	7		9					
	9	4		8				
		2	4		3		1	
		7				2		
	5		2		1	7		
				5		4	8	
					9		7	3
	3					9		

EXPERT

PUZZLE 66

9			8					
	1	7			6		9	
		3				4		
	9			6			8	
	5		1		3		6	
	3			7			2	
	5					9		
	8		9			5	3	
					4			1

EXPERT

PUZZLE 67

						1		
				5	2			6
	4	8	9					5
3	1			4			5	
		9				7		
	2			7			1	8
5					7	2	8	
2			4	9				
		3						

EXPERT

PUZZLE 68

			7			9		
				9				
			8	2	4	7		3
6	2					1	9	
		3				5		
	1	8					7	2
3		5	6	1	8			
				3				
		6			2			

EXPERT

PUZZLE 69

7								
			3	8			5	
		9	2				3	4
						2		
	5		1	2	8		9	
		7						
6	2				5	1		
	9			4	3			
								5

EXPERT

PUZZLE 70

		2		5		7		
		1					6	2
9				8				
			3					7
	1		5	9	7		8	
2					6			
				4				6
8	5					3		
		6		7		9		

EXPERT

				7		3		
	9			2		4		1
			4			6		
	5						9	
9			1		3			4
	2					7		
		9			2			
5		3		6			8	
		1		3				

EXPERT

PUZZLE 72

				4		1		
	8	5	6			2		
2								7
	9				8	6		
8			7		5			3
		6	9				1	
6								2
		8			9	5	4	
		2	7					

EXPERT

PUZZLE 73

4	9			6		1		
		2				4		
6	1						9	
	7			9	3			
8								2
			1	5			4	
	4						7	1
		7				2		
		6		3			5	4

EXPERT

PUZZLE 74

				7	8			9
	1		9					
9						3	4	
		6		9			5	
			7	6	2			
	4			5		1		
	2	8						6
					7		3	
5			3	4				

EXPERT

PUZZLE 75

9	3					6		4
				2			9	3
1	4		9					
8	1			5				
				4			6	5
					8		3	2
2	5			7				
6		3					4	9

EXPERT

PUZZLE 76

			8	7		9		
	6				3		7	
				6		5	3	
						7	1	3
		6				8		
7	9	4						
	7	9		2				
2			4				8	
		8		1	6			

EXPERT

PUZZLE 77

8			1					
		2		8	3	6		
	1		6		2			5
	2		4					
	9					3		
				7			6	
4			7		1		5	
		5	3	2		8		
				8				9

EXPERT

PUZZLE 78

		3		5	8	7		
		4						3
	6		1				2	8
3	5							
				2				
							7	5
6	7				5		3	
8						9		
		2	6	4		5		

EXPERT

PUZZLE 79

6			8		1	7		2
		1		6	9			
	1	7				6		
	2			3			4	
		4				2	8	
			5	4		3		
5		2	1		6			9

EXPERT

PUZZLE 80

			6	1		4		5
						8		
				7			3	6
			2	1	7			
4	9						2	8
	8	5	9					
5	1	9						
	2							
9	3		6	2				

EXPERT

LARGE PRINT SUDOKU

ANSWER PAGES

PUZZLE 1 | PAGE 3

7	4	6	9	2	3	8	1	5
3	2	8	4	5	1	9	7	6
1	9	5	6	7	8	4	3	2
9	3	7	2	8	4	6	5	1
6	8	4	3	1	5	2	9	7
5	1	2	7	9	6	3	4	8
4	5	3	8	6	7	1	2	9
2	6	1	5	4	9	7	8	3
8	7	9	1	3	2	5	6	4

PUZZLE 2 | PAGE 4

2	1	4	3	7	9	8	6	5
6	5	9	4	8	1	7	3	2
7	3	8	2	6	5	4	1	9
9	8	3	1	5	6	2	4	7
5	6	7	9	4	2	3	8	1
1	4	2	8	3	7	5	9	6
8	7	1	5	9	3	6	2	4
3	9	6	7	2	4	1	5	8
4	2	5	6	1	8	9	7	3

PUZZLE 3 | PAGE 5

4	1	9	6	5	2	3	8	7
3	5	7	8	9	4	2	1	6
2	6	8	1	7	3	5	9	4
1	3	6	5	4	8	7	2	9
8	9	5	2	6	7	4	3	1
7	2	4	3	1	9	6	5	8
5	4	3	9	8	6	1	7	2
9	7	2	4	3	1	8	6	5
6	8	1	7	2	5	9	4	3

PUZZLE 4 | PAGE 6

4	1	3	9	2	6	8	7	5
7	9	5	1	8	4	3	6	2
6	8	2	3	7	5	9	4	1
2	7	9	5	6	1	4	8	3
3	5	8	4	9	2	6	1	7
1	4	6	7	3	8	5	2	9
9	2	4	6	5	7	1	3	8
5	6	7	8	1	3	2	9	4
8	3	1	2	4	9	7	5	6

PUZZLE 5 | PAGE 7

2	6	1	3	4	8	7	9	5
3	4	7	6	5	9	1	8	2
9	8	5	7	2	1	4	6	3
7	2	6	1	9	3	8	5	4
5	3	8	2	7	4	6	1	9
4	1	9	5	8	6	2	3	7
1	7	3	4	6	5	9	2	8
8	5	4	9	1	2	3	7	6
6	9	2	8	3	7	5	4	1

PUZZLE 6 | PAGE 8

6	5	8	4	9	1	7	2	3
4	3	1	5	7	2	8	9	6
7	2	9	6	3	8	4	5	1
3	6	4	2	1	7	9	8	5
2	9	7	8	6	5	1	3	4
1	8	5	3	4	9	2	6	7
8	1	6	9	5	4	3	7	2
9	4	3	7	2	6	5	1	8
5	7	2	1	8	3	6	4	9

PUZZLE 7 | PAGE 9

7	2	8	1	5	3	4	6	9
9	3	4	7	8	6	2	5	1
1	6	5	9	4	2	3	8	7
2	7	3	8	6	9	5	1	4
5	9	1	3	2	4	8	7	6
4	8	6	5	1	7	9	3	2
6	5	9	4	7	8	1	2	3
3	1	7	2	9	5	6	4	8
8	4	2	6	3	1	7	9	5

PUZZLE 8 | PAGE 10

2	5	8	4	6	9	1	3	7
9	4	6	3	1	7	5	2	8
7	1	3	5	8	2	4	6	9
4	6	7	8	9	3	2	1	5
1	8	2	7	4	5	6	9	3
5	3	9	1	2	6	8	7	4
3	2	5	6	7	4	9	8	1
6	7	1	9	5	8	3	4	2
8	9	4	2	3	1	7	5	6

PUZZLE 9 | PAGE 11

1	2	9	5	7	6	3	4	8
6	4	5	3	9	8	7	2	1
8	7	3	4	2	1	9	5	6
7	5	1	8	6	4	2	3	9
4	8	2	1	3	9	6	7	5
9	3	6	7	5	2	8	1	4
3	6	4	9	1	7	5	8	2
2	1	7	6	8	5	4	9	3
5	9	8	2	4	3	1	6	7

PUZZLE 10 | PAGE 12

7	8	1	3	4	6	9	5	2
9	5	4	2	7	8	6	3	1
3	2	6	1	5	9	8	4	7
8	9	2	7	3	5	1	6	4
6	1	5	9	2	4	7	8	3
4	7	3	8	6	1	5	2	9
2	3	8	6	9	7	4	1	5
1	4	9	5	8	2	3	7	6
5	6	7	4	1	3	2	9	8

PUZZLE 11 | PAGE 13

4	1	6	5	2	7	9	8	3
9	2	8	1	4	3	7	6	5
3	5	7	8	9	6	4	2	1
6	4	2	7	1	9	5	3	8
7	3	5	4	6	8	1	9	2
8	9	1	2	3	5	6	7	4
2	7	9	3	5	4	8	1	6
1	6	4	9	8	2	3	5	7
5	8	3	6	7	1	2	4	9

PUZZLE 12 | PAGE 14

6	5	7	3	8	1	2	9	4
9	4	1	6	5	2	8	7	3
8	3	2	9	7	4	6	1	5
3	9	8	2	1	5	4	6	7
7	2	5	4	6	3	9	8	1
4	1	6	8	9	7	5	3	2
5	6	3	7	2	8	1	4	9
1	8	4	5	3	9	7	2	6
2	7	9	1	4	6	3	5	8

PUZZLE 13 | PAGE 15

2	6	5	3	4	8	1	9	7
4	1	8	9	6	7	5	3	2
9	3	7	5	2	1	8	4	6
1	9	4	8	7	2	3	6	5
7	2	6	1	3	5	9	8	4
8	5	3	4	9	6	7	2	1
6	8	2	7	5	9	4	1	3
3	7	1	6	8	4	2	5	9
5	4	9	2	1	3	6	7	8

PUZZLE 14 | PAGE 16

5	8	4	7	9	2	1	3	6
9	7	3	5	6	1	2	4	8
2	1	6	3	4	8	7	5	9
6	5	2	9	8	7	3	1	4
4	3	1	6	2	5	8	9	7
7	9	8	1	3	4	6	2	5
3	6	5	2	7	9	4	8	1
1	4	7	8	5	3	9	6	2
8	2	9	4	1	6	5	7	3

PUZZLE 15 | PAGE 17

3	9	1	2	4	6	7	8	5
8	7	2	5	1	9	6	4	3
4	6	5	7	8	3	2	1	9
7	4	9	6	3	5	1	2	8
5	1	6	8	9	2	3	7	4
2	3	8	4	7	1	5	9	6
1	2	3	9	6	8	4	5	7
9	5	4	3	2	7	8	6	1
6	8	7	1	5	4	9	3	2

PUZZLE 16 | PAGE 18

5	2	6	8	1	9	7	4	3
7	4	9	3	2	6	8	5	1
3	8	1	5	7	4	6	2	9
2	9	4	7	6	5	1	3	8
6	1	3	9	4	8	5	7	2
8	5	7	2	3	1	9	6	4
1	6	5	4	9	2	3	8	7
9	7	2	6	8	3	4	1	5
4	3	8	1	5	7	2	9	6

PUZZLE 17 | PAGE 19

8	3	5	4	2	1	9	7	6
4	6	7	8	3	9	1	5	2
9	2	1	6	5	7	8	4	3
7	1	9	2	6	4	5	3	8
3	8	2	7	1	5	4	6	9
6	5	4	9	8	3	7	2	1
1	7	3	5	9	2	6	8	4
5	9	6	3	4	8	2	1	7
2	4	8	1	7	6	3	9	5

PUZZLE 18 | PAGE 20

5	7	3	9	2	8	6	1	4
2	9	1	7	4	6	5	8	3
4	6	8	5	1	3	2	7	9
3	8	4	2	6	5	1	9	7
9	1	5	4	3	7	8	6	2
7	2	6	8	9	1	4	3	5
6	3	2	1	5	9	7	4	8
8	5	9	6	7	4	3	2	1
1	4	7	3	8	2	9	5	6

PUZZLE 19 | PAGE 21

8	3	7	4	6	5	1	2	9
9	5	1	8	2	3	4	6	7
2	4	6	1	9	7	3	5	8
1	6	5	3	7	9	2	8	4
7	9	4	2	8	6	5	1	3
3	2	8	5	4	1	7	9	6
5	7	3	6	1	8	9	4	2
4	8	9	7	5	2	6	3	1
6	1	2	9	3	4	8	7	5

PUZZLE 20 | PAGE 22

2	5	1	8	9	3	4	6	7
8	7	3	2	4	6	1	5	9
4	6	9	5	1	7	3	2	8
5	3	2	7	6	8	9	4	1
6	4	8	1	5	9	2	7	3
1	9	7	3	2	4	5	8	6
9	1	4	6	7	2	8	3	5
7	8	5	4	3	1	6	9	2
3	2	6	9	8	5	7	1	4

PUZZLE 21 | PAGE 23

1	7	6	4	3	9	2	5	8
9	5	8	1	2	6	4	7	3
2	3	4	8	7	5	9	6	1
6	1	3	7	8	2	5	9	4
5	4	2	9	6	1	3	8	7
7	8	9	3	5	4	6	1	2
3	9	7	5	4	8	1	2	6
8	6	5	2	1	3	7	4	9
4	2	1	6	9	7	8	3	5

PUZZLE 22 | PAGE 24

6	7	9	4	8	5	2	3	1
5	8	1	3	6	2	9	7	4
3	2	4	9	1	7	6	5	8
4	9	8	2	7	1	3	6	5
1	3	6	5	9	8	4	2	7
7	5	2	6	4	3	8	1	9
9	6	7	1	2	4	5	8	3
2	1	3	8	5	9	7	4	6
8	4	5	7	3	6	1	9	2

3	7	6	2	5	9	4	1	8
5	9	1	4	7	8	6	2	3
4	2	8	6	1	3	9	5	7
2	6	7	8	4	5	3	9	1
9	3	5	7	6	1	8	4	2
8	1	4	3	9	2	7	6	5
6	5	9	1	3	7	2	8	4
1	8	3	9	2	4	5	7	6
7	4	2	5	8	6	1	3	9

2	8	1	9	4	3	6	7	5
5	4	7	6	8	2	1	9	3
6	3	9	7	5	1	4	8	2
9	6	4	3	7	8	2	5	1
7	5	3	1	2	9	8	4	6
1	2	8	5	6	4	7	3	9
3	7	6	8	1	5	9	2	4
8	9	2	4	3	6	5	1	7
4	1	5	2	9	7	3	6	8

3	1	2	6	5	4	8	7	9
7	9	6	3	2	8	4	1	5
5	8	4	7	9	1	2	6	3
2	3	9	8	1	6	5	4	7
8	4	5	9	7	2	1	3	6
1	6	7	5	4	3	9	8	2
9	7	8	1	6	5	3	2	4
6	2	1	4	3	9	7	5	8
4	5	3	2	8	7	6	9	1

6	5	3	9	2	8	4	7	1
1	7	4	5	6	3	8	2	9
2	9	8	7	1	4	5	6	3
5	2	9	6	8	1	3	4	7
8	3	6	4	7	5	1	9	2
7	4	1	3	9	2	6	8	5
3	8	5	2	4	7	9	1	6
4	6	2	1	5	9	7	3	8
9	1	7	8	3	6	2	5	4

7	1	3	6	5	9	8	2	4
8	5	6	2	4	3	9	1	7
4	2	9	7	8	1	6	3	5
2	7	8	1	3	5	4	6	9
3	6	1	9	7	4	2	5	8
5	9	4	8	2	6	1	7	3
1	4	5	3	6	8	7	9	2
9	3	2	4	1	7	5	8	6
6	8	7	5	9	2	3	4	1

9	3	7	6	5	8	1	2	4
5	1	6	9	2	4	7	8	3
2	8	4	3	7	1	9	6	5
7	5	3	8	9	2	6	4	1
6	9	8	4	1	5	3	7	2
4	2	1	7	3	6	5	9	8
8	7	5	1	4	9	2	3	6
3	6	2	5	8	7	4	1	9
1	4	9	2	6	3	8	5	7

6	8	1	2	7	4	5	9	3
4	3	9	5	6	1	2	7	8
5	2	7	9	8	3	6	1	4
1	9	8	3	4	5	7	2	6
2	6	3	1	9	7	8	4	5
7	5	4	6	2	8	1	3	9
8	4	2	7	3	6	9	5	1
3	7	5	8	1	9	4	6	2
9	1	6	4	5	2	3	8	7

6	5	4	2	3	9	8	7	1
1	8	9	7	6	4	2	3	5
3	2	7	5	1	8	4	9	6
2	7	6	9	8	1	5	4	3
9	3	1	4	5	2	6	8	7
8	4	5	6	7	3	1	2	9
4	9	3	1	2	5	7	6	8
7	1	8	3	4	6	9	5	2
5	6	2	8	9	7	3	1	4

8	6	9	4	7	1	5	3	2
5	3	1	8	9	2	4	6	7
2	4	7	6	3	5	8	9	1
1	5	8	7	6	3	2	4	9
6	9	4	2	5	8	1	7	3
7	2	3	1	4	9	6	8	5
3	7	2	5	8	6	9	1	4
4	8	5	9	1	7	3	2	6
9	1	6	3	2	4	7	5	8

2	8	7	5	3	4	1	9	6
6	9	5	8	1	2	4	3	7
3	4	1	6	7	9	2	5	8
4	7	6	1	2	3	9	8	5
5	1	9	4	6	8	7	2	3
8	2	3	9	5	7	6	4	1
1	3	2	7	4	5	8	6	9
7	5	8	2	9	6	3	1	4
9	6	4	3	8	1	5	7	2

5	2	3	6	1	7	9	8	4
6	8	1	4	9	3	7	5	2
4	9	7	2	5	8	3	1	6
9	5	8	3	7	2	4	6	1
1	3	4	8	6	5	2	7	9
7	6	2	1	4	9	5	3	8
3	1	9	5	8	4	6	2	7
8	4	5	7	2	6	1	9	3
2	7	6	9	3	1	8	4	5

9	6	1	4	8	2	7	3	5
4	5	8	7	9	3	6	1	2
2	3	7	5	1	6	8	4	9
5	7	4	2	3	9	1	8	6
6	8	9	1	4	7	5	2	3
3	1	2	8	6	5	4	9	7
8	9	3	6	7	4	2	5	1
7	4	5	9	2	1	3	6	8
1	2	6	3	5	8	9	7	4

PUZZLE 35 | PAGE 37

7	4	8	1	9	6	5	3	2
2	3	9	8	4	5	7	1	6
5	1	6	7	3	2	8	9	4
3	7	5	9	1	4	2	6	8
4	8	2	5	6	3	1	7	9
9	6	1	2	8	7	3	4	5
8	9	3	4	2	1	6	5	7
1	5	4	6	7	8	9	2	3
6	2	7	3	5	9	4	8	1

PUZZLE 36 | PAGE 38

7	4	2	9	8	5	3	1	6
6	5	9	3	2	1	7	8	4
1	3	8	4	6	7	5	9	2
3	1	6	7	9	8	2	4	5
9	8	5	2	4	3	6	7	1
2	7	4	5	1	6	9	3	8
4	2	3	8	5	9	1	6	7
8	6	7	1	3	2	4	5	9
5	9	1	6	7	4	8	2	3

PUZZLE 37 | PAGE 39

9	6	5	7	8	2	1	3	4
4	2	1	5	6	3	7	8	9
8	7	3	9	1	4	2	6	5
5	4	6	2	3	9	8	7	1
2	1	9	8	7	5	3	4	6
7	3	8	6	4	1	5	9	2
1	9	4	3	5	8	6	2	7
3	5	7	4	2	6	9	1	8
6	8	2	1	9	7	4	5	3

PUZZLE 38 | PAGE 40

7	8	5	3	1	9	4	2	6
1	9	6	4	8	2	5	7	3
2	4	3	6	7	5	1	8	9
3	1	9	2	4	8	7	6	5
5	6	4	7	9	1	8	3	2
8	7	2	5	3	6	9	1	4
9	2	1	8	5	3	6	4	7
4	3	8	9	6	7	2	5	1
6	5	7	1	2	4	3	9	8

PUZZLE 39 | PAGE 41

1	6	4	8	2	9	5	7	3
8	3	2	5	6	7	4	9	1
9	7	5	1	3	4	6	8	2
3	2	8	7	9	6	1	5	4
6	5	7	4	8	1	3	2	9
4	1	9	3	5	2	7	6	8
5	8	6	2	1	3	9	4	7
7	9	3	6	4	8	2	1	5
2	4	1	9	7	5	8	3	6

PUZZLE 40 | PAGE 42

5	7	3	4	1	6	2	9	8
9	2	6	5	8	3	1	4	7
8	4	1	9	2	7	5	3	6
2	3	7	6	4	8	9	5	1
1	6	9	7	3	5	4	8	2
4	5	8	2	9	1	6	7	3
6	9	4	8	7	2	3	1	5
3	8	5	1	6	4	7	2	9
7	1	2	3	5	9	8	6	4

2	1	6	9	3	5	7	8	4
7	3	9	8	4	2	6	1	5
5	8	4	6	1	7	2	9	3
6	2	1	4	5	9	8	3	7
3	9	5	7	6	8	1	4	2
8	4	7	3	2	1	5	6	9
4	5	8	1	7	3	9	2	6
9	6	2	5	8	4	3	7	1
1	7	3	2	9	6	4	5	8

8	9	5	2	6	7	1	4	3
3	4	6	5	9	1	7	8	2
2	7	1	8	3	4	9	5	6
7	1	2	4	8	5	6	3	9
5	3	8	6	1	9	2	7	4
9	6	4	7	2	3	8	1	5
4	8	7	9	5	2	3	6	1
1	5	9	3	7	6	4	2	8
6	2	3	1	4	8	5	9	7

5	1	8	6	4	9	7	2	3
4	9	6	3	2	7	8	1	5
3	7	2	8	1	5	9	4	6
8	2	3	7	6	4	5	9	1
1	4	5	2	9	3	6	7	8
9	6	7	1	5	8	4	3	2
6	5	9	4	3	2	1	8	7
2	8	4	5	7	1	3	6	9
7	3	1	9	8	6	2	5	4

4	8	1	6	2	3	7	9	5
2	6	7	9	4	5	1	3	8
5	9	3	7	1	8	4	2	6
1	7	5	4	6	9	3	8	2
8	2	4	3	5	1	6	7	9
6	3	9	8	7	2	5	1	4
7	1	2	5	9	6	8	4	3
9	5	8	1	3	4	2	6	7
3	4	6	2	8	7	9	5	1

5	4	8	2	6	1	3	9	7
3	2	6	9	7	8	4	1	5
1	9	7	4	3	5	2	8	6
8	7	2	6	5	9	1	3	4
9	3	4	1	2	7	6	5	8
6	5	1	8	4	3	9	7	2
7	6	3	5	1	4	8	2	9
2	1	9	7	8	6	5	4	3
4	8	5	3	9	2	7	6	1

7	2	3	1	8	5	6	4	9
6	5	9	4	3	7	8	2	1
8	1	4	9	6	2	5	3	7
9	6	7	3	2	1	4	8	5
3	4	1	7	5	8	2	9	6
2	8	5	6	4	9	7	1	3
5	3	6	8	1	4	9	7	2
1	7	8	2	9	6	3	5	4
4	9	2	5	7	3	1	6	8

1	9	2	8	7	5	4	6	3
3	4	8	6	2	9	1	7	5
5	7	6	4	1	3	9	2	8
9	1	5	7	3	2	8	4	6
6	2	4	5	8	1	7	3	9
8	3	7	9	6	4	2	5	1
2	6	9	1	5	7	3	8	4
4	8	3	2	9	6	5	1	7
7	5	1	3	4	8	6	9	2

PUZZLE 48 | PAGE 50

6	5	2	9	8	3	7	4	1
9	8	1	4	7	6	3	5	2
7	3	4	5	1	2	6	9	8
8	9	3	2	6	5	1	7	4
5	2	7	3	4	1	9	8	6
4	1	6	8	9	7	5	2	3
3	6	5	7	2	8	4	1	9
2	7	9	1	3	4	8	6	5
1	4	8	6	5	9	2	3	7

PUZZLE 49 | PAGE 51

6	3	5	8	7	1	4	2	9
1	9	2	3	4	5	8	7	6
7	8	4	9	2	6	5	1	3
4	7	8	5	6	9	2	3	1
9	2	1	7	3	4	6	8	5
5	6	3	1	8	2	7	9	4
3	4	6	2	1	7	9	5	8
8	5	7	6	9	3	1	4	2
2	1	9	4	5	8	3	6	7

PUZZLE 50 | PAGE 52

6	9	4	3	1	7	8	5	2
3	5	2	6	8	4	7	1	9
1	7	8	5	9	2	6	3	4
2	8	1	9	7	5	3	4	6
4	6	9	1	2	3	5	7	8
7	3	5	4	6	8	9	2	1
5	2	3	8	4	9	1	6	7
9	1	7	2	3	6	4	8	5
8	4	6	7	5	1	2	9	3

PUZZLE 51 | PAGE 53

6	7	8	9	5	3	2	1	4
2	9	1	7	8	4	3	5	6
3	4	5	2	6	1	7	8	9
1	5	2	3	9	6	4	7	8
4	8	6	5	2	7	9	3	1
9	3	7	4	1	8	5	6	2
7	1	4	6	3	9	8	2	5
8	2	3	1	4	5	6	9	7
5	6	9	8	7	2	1	4	3

PUZZLE 52 | PAGE 54

9	3	2	1	7	5	4	8	6
1	7	8	4	6	3	9	2	5
6	4	5	8	9	2	7	3	1
7	9	6	5	3	4	2	1	8
8	5	4	7	2	1	3	6	9
2	1	3	9	8	6	5	7	4
5	2	7	6	4	8	1	9	3
4	6	9	3	1	7	8	5	2
3	8	1	2	5	9	6	4	7

5	3	2	6	1	8	7	9	4
4	6	9	7	5	2	3	8	1
7	8	1	3	9	4	6	5	2
9	7	8	4	6	3	1	2	5
6	1	3	2	8	5	9	4	7
2	5	4	9	7	1	8	6	3
1	2	5	8	3	9	4	7	6
3	9	7	5	4	6	2	1	8
8	4	6	1	2	7	5	3	9

7	3	9	1	6	4	8	2	5
4	5	2	8	7	3	9	1	6
8	1	6	5	9	2	3	4	7
6	7	8	2	4	5	1	3	9
3	4	5	9	1	6	7	8	2
2	9	1	3	8	7	5	6	4
9	6	3	4	5	1	2	7	8
1	8	4	7	2	9	6	5	3
5	2	7	6	3	8	4	9	1

8	9	2	1	6	5	7	3	4
7	5	4	8	2	3	1	9	6
6	1	3	9	4	7	8	2	5
9	2	6	7	5	8	3	4	1
3	8	5	4	9	1	2	6	7
4	7	1	2	3	6	9	5	8
2	4	7	5	1	9	6	8	3
1	3	9	6	8	4	5	7	2
5	6	8	3	7	2	4	1	9

4	2	6	8	1	7	5	9	3
9	8	3	4	5	2	6	1	7
5	7	1	3	9	6	2	4	8
1	9	7	6	2	4	3	8	5
2	5	8	1	7	3	4	6	9
6	3	4	5	8	9	1	7	2
3	1	9	7	4	5	8	2	6
7	4	5	2	6	8	9	3	1
8	6	2	9	3	1	7	5	4

1	6	7	8	5	9	3	2	4
5	3	9	4	2	7	6	8	1
4	2	8	1	6	3	9	5	7
3	1	2	9	7	8	4	6	5
6	7	4	2	3	5	1	9	8
9	8	5	6	4	1	7	3	2
2	5	3	7	1	6	8	4	9
7	9	6	5	8	4	2	1	3
8	4	1	3	9	2	5	7	6

3	8	9	1	7	4	2	5	6
4	5	7	2	3	6	9	8	1
2	6	1	8	9	5	4	3	7
5	4	8	7	6	2	1	9	3
9	1	2	4	8	3	7	6	5
6	7	3	9	5	1	8	2	4
7	2	5	3	4	8	6	1	9
1	9	6	5	2	7	3	4	8
8	3	4	6	1	9	5	7	2

PUZZLE 59 | PAGE 61

9	1	5	6	8	4	2	7	3
3	4	7	2	5	9	8	6	1
6	8	2	1	7	3	4	9	5
2	5	1	4	9	7	6	3	8
7	3	8	5	6	1	9	2	4
4	6	9	8	3	2	1	5	7
8	2	6	3	1	5	7	4	9
5	7	4	9	2	8	3	1	6
1	9	3	7	4	6	5	8	2

PUZZLE 60 | PAGE 62

7	1	2	5	9	3	6	8	4
4	5	8	7	1	6	9	2	3
9	3	6	4	2	8	1	5	7
6	9	5	8	7	2	3	4	1
8	2	7	1	3	4	5	9	6
3	4	1	6	5	9	8	7	2
2	8	3	9	6	7	4	1	5
1	6	4	2	8	5	7	3	9
5	7	9	3	4	1	2	6	8

PUZZLE 61 | PAGE 63

1	5	6	8	9	3	4	7	2
2	3	8	7	1	4	9	6	5
7	4	9	5	6	2	8	1	3
9	1	4	6	3	7	5	2	8
3	6	5	2	8	9	7	4	1
8	2	7	4	5	1	3	9	6
6	7	3	1	4	8	2	5	9
4	9	1	3	2	5	6	8	7
5	8	2	9	7	6	1	3	4

PUZZLE 62 | PAGE 64

6	1	5	8	3	2	4	9	7
2	4	3	9	1	7	5	6	8
7	8	9	5	6	4	1	3	2
4	6	2	3	9	1	8	7	5
8	9	1	7	5	6	3	2	4
5	3	7	2	4	8	9	1	6
3	2	6	4	8	9	7	5	1
9	7	4	1	2	5	6	8	3
1	5	8	6	7	3	2	4	9

PUZZLE 63 | PAGE 65

1	6	3	9	7	2	5	4	8
5	9	2	1	8	4	3	6	7
7	8	4	6	3	5	2	9	1
8	4	1	5	2	3	9	7	6
6	2	7	8	4	9	1	5	3
3	5	9	7	6	1	8	2	4
9	1	8	4	5	6	7	3	2
2	7	6	3	9	8	4	1	5
4	3	5	2	1	7	6	8	9

PUZZLE 64 | PAGE 66

3	7	5	9	6	4	8	2	1
6	4	8	1	2	5	9	3	7
1	9	2	3	7	8	5	4	6
7	5	6	2	9	1	4	8	3
8	3	4	7	5	6	2	1	9
2	1	9	8	4	3	7	6	5
9	6	3	4	8	7	1	5	2
5	8	7	6	1	2	3	9	4
4	2	1	5	3	9	6	7	8

PUZZLE 65 | PAGE 67

3	1	8	7	4	2	6	5	9
2	7	6	9	3	5	1	4	8
5	9	4	1	8	6	3	2	7
9	6	2	4	7	3	8	1	5
1	4	7	5	9	8	2	3	6
8	5	3	2	6	1	7	9	4
6	2	9	3	5	7	4	8	1
4	8	1	6	2	9	5	7	3
7	3	5	8	1	4	9	6	2

PUZZLE 66 | PAGE 68

9	4	2	8	3	1	6	5	7
8	1	7	5	4	6	2	9	3
5	6	3	7	9	2	4	1	8
7	9	1	2	6	5	3	8	4
2	5	4	1	8	3	7	6	9
6	3	8	4	7	9	1	2	5
1	7	5	3	2	8	9	4	6
4	8	6	9	1	7	5	3	2
3	2	9	6	5	4	8	7	1

PUZZLE 67 | PAGE 69

6	5	2	8	3	4	1	9	7
9	3	1	7	5	2	8	4	6
7	4	8	9	1	6	3	2	5
3	1	7	6	4	8	9	5	2
8	6	9	5	2	1	7	3	4
4	2	5	3	7	9	6	1	8
5	9	4	1	6	7	2	8	3
2	8	6	4	9	3	5	7	1
1	7	3	2	8	5	4	6	9

PUZZLE 68 | PAGE 70

8	3	2	7	6	5	9	1	4
4	6	7	1	9	3	2	8	5
1	5	9	8	2	4	7	6	3
6	2	4	3	5	7	1	9	8
7	9	3	2	8	1	5	4	6
5	1	8	9	4	6	3	7	2
3	7	5	6	1	8	4	2	9
2	8	1	4	3	9	6	5	7
9	4	6	5	7	2	8	3	1

PUZZLE 69 | PAGE 71

7	3	1	5	9	4	6	2	8
4	6	2	3	8	7	9	5	1
5	8	9	2	6	1	7	3	4
9	4	8	7	5	6	2	1	3
3	5	6	1	2	8	4	9	7
2	1	7	4	3	9	5	8	6
6	2	3	8	7	5	1	4	9
1	9	5	6	4	3	8	7	2
8	7	4	9	1	2	3	6	5

PUZZLE 70 | PAGE 72

3	4	2	6	5	1	7	9	8
5	8	1	7	3	9	4	6	2
9	6	7	2	8	4	1	5	3
4	9	5	3	2	8	6	1	7
6	1	3	5	9	7	2	8	4
2	7	8	4	1	6	5	3	9
7	3	9	1	4	5	8	2	6
8	5	4	9	6	2	3	7	1
1	2	6	8	7	3	9	4	5

PUZZLE 71 | PAGE 73

4	5	6	8	7	1	3	2	9
7	9	8	3	2	6	4	5	1
1	3	2	4	9	5	6	7	8
6	1	5	2	4	7	8	9	3
9	8	7	1	5	3	2	6	4
3	2	4	6	8	9	7	1	5
8	4	9	7	1	2	5	3	6
5	7	3	9	6	4	1	8	2
2	6	1	5	3	8	9	4	7

PUZZLE 72 | PAGE 74

7	6	3	8	4	2	1	5	9
1	8	5	6	9	7	2	3	4
2	4	9	3	5	1	8	6	7
4	9	7	1	3	8	6	2	5
8	2	1	7	6	5	4	9	3
5	3	6	9	2	4	7	1	8
6	1	4	5	8	3	9	7	2
3	7	8	2	1	9	5	4	6
9	5	2	4	7	6	3	8	1

PUZZLE 73 | PAGE 75

4	9	5	3	6	8	1	2	7
7	3	2	9	1	5	4	8	6
6	1	8	4	2	7	5	9	3
2	7	4	8	9	3	6	1	5
8	5	1	6	7	4	9	3	2
9	6	3	1	5	2	7	4	8
5	4	9	2	8	6	3	7	1
3	8	7	5	4	1	2	6	9
1	2	6	7	3	9	8	5	4

PUZZLE 74 | PAGE 76

6	3	2	4	7	8	5	1	9
8	1	4	9	3	5	6	2	7
9	7	5	6	2	1	3	4	8
2	8	6	1	9	4	7	5	3
1	5	3	7	6	2	8	9	4
7	4	9	8	5	3	1	6	2
3	2	8	5	1	9	4	7	6
4	6	1	2	8	7	9	3	5
5	9	7	3	4	6	2	8	1

PUZZLE 75 | PAGE 77

9	3	2	1	8	7	6	5	4
7	6	8	5	2	4	1	9	3
1	4	5	9	3	6	2	7	8
8	1	6	3	5	9	4	2	7
5	9	4	7	6	2	3	8	1
3	2	7	8	4	1	9	6	5
4	7	1	6	9	8	5	3	2
2	5	9	4	7	3	8	1	6
6	8	3	2	1	5	7	4	9

PUZZLE 76 | PAGE 78

2	4	3	8	7	5	9	6	1
5	6	1	2	9	3	4	7	8
9	8	7	1	6	4	5	3	2
8	5	2	6	4	9	7	1	3
3	1	6	7	5	2	8	9	4
7	9	4	3	8	1	6	2	5
1	7	9	5	2	8	3	4	6
6	2	5	4	3	7	1	8	9
4	3	8	9	1	6	2	5	7

PUZZLE 77 | PAGE 79

8	6	7	1	5	4	9	3	2
5	4	2	9	8	3	6	1	7
9	1	3	6	7	2	4	8	5
6	2	1	4	3	5	7	9	8
7	5	9	8	1	6	3	2	4
3	8	4	2	9	7	5	6	1
4	9	8	7	6	1	2	5	3
1	7	5	3	2	9	8	4	6
2	3	6	5	4	8	1	7	9

PUZZLE 78 | PAGE 80

2	1	3	4	5	8	7	6	9
9	8	4	2	6	7	1	5	3
5	6	7	1	9	3	4	2	8
3	5	1	7	8	4	6	9	2
7	9	8	5	2	6	3	4	1
4	2	6	9	3	1	8	7	5
6	7	9	8	1	5	2	3	4
8	4	5	3	7	2	9	1	6
1	3	2	6	4	9	5	8	7

PUZZLE 79 | PAGE 81

2	9	8	3	7	4	5	1	6
6	4	3	8	5	1	7	9	2
7	5	1	2	6	9	8	3	4
9	1	7	4	2	8	6	5	3
8	2	5	6	3	7	9	4	1
3	6	4	9	1	5	2	8	7
1	7	9	5	4	2	3	6	8
5	3	2	1	8	6	4	7	9
4	8	6	7	9	3	1	2	5

PUZZLE 80 | PAGE 82

8	2	7	6	1	3	4	9	5
3	4	6	2	5	9	8	1	7
1	5	9	4	8	7	2	3	6
6	3	5	8	2	1	7	4	9
4	9	1	3	7	6	5	2	8
2	7	8	5	9	4	3	6	1
5	1	4	9	3	8	6	7	2
7	6	2	1	4	5	9	8	3
9	8	3	7	6	2	1	5	4

LOOK FOR MORE PAPP PUZZLE BOOKS!

www.pappintl.com